Born in London Penelope Alexander moved from there to Spain as a young girl, being referred as 'the girl with itchy feet'. Life went on and after her divorce she met her second husband who was the light of her life. He died very suddenly which left her heartbroken. She decided life in the UK was unbearable without him so she contacted a friend in South Africa. Penelope then opened her own restaurant in Cape Town called 'The Poet's Cusine.'

To my daughter, Robyn, and my son, Mark, who have stood like sentinels, unwavering in their belief in my writing. Their encouragement has been instrumental in the creation of this book. Lastly, but certainly not least, my grandson Elliott, whose talents as a graphic designer brought the book's cover to life. I am immensely proud of him.

Penelope Alexander

PENNY'S POEMS

AUSTIN MACAULEY PUBLISHERS™
LONDON • CAMBRIDGE • NEW YORK • SHARJAH

Copyright © Penelope Alexander 2024

The right of Penelope Alexander to be identified as author of this work has been asserted by the author in accordance with sections 77 and 78 of the Copyright, Designs and Patents Act 1988.

All rights reserved. No part of this publication may be reproduced, stored in a retrieval system, or transmitted in any form or by any means, electronic, mechanical, photocopying, recording, or otherwise, without the prior permission of the publishers.

Any person who commits any unauthorised act in relation to this publication may be liable to criminal prosecution and civil claims for damages.

A CIP catalogue record for this title is available from the British Library.

ISBN 9781035848201 (Paperback)
ISBN 9781035848218 (ePub e-book)

www.austinmacauley.com

First Published 2024
Austin Macauley Publishers Ltd®
1 Canada Square
Canary Wharf
London
E14 5AA

I would like to thank Austin Macauley publishers for giving me the opportunity of sharing my poems with others.

Winter

Winter creeps with stealthy hand
Cold winds sweep this barren land.
The sun with watery filter streams
And summer is lost with all her dreams.

November nights, December days
The harvest moon has lost its rays.
Jack Frost will bite the cold night air
With icy fingers bright and bare.

With log fire burning bright and gold,
And tales of long, told of old,
Winter creeps but the night is warm
We are protected from the storm.

A Poet's Palette

Do you ever sit and dream that things are never what they seem?
The sky has turned dark navy blue; the clouds have a golden hue.
The grass is deepest purple now with red buttercups that sway and bow.
The trees bear leaves of darkest night; such things will startle you with fright.

The stream that gurgles with pretty song, seems to know there is something wrong
The bluebells now bear an emerald green as they stand tall beside the stream.
The squirrel is confused to know, his nuts now bear a pinkish glow.
The poet's pen can change this land; it gives food for thought to those at hand.

A Walk in the Woods

What is that just near that tree, with bright brown eyes he stares at me?
His crown of antlers he regally wears, yet so still he stands and simply stares.
His Majesty he wears with pride, even though he cannot hide.
I move with stealth but he takes fright, he springs to life, and is gone from sight.

I wander through the woods and beam; you are not alone for long it seems.
A rabbit pops out his little head; I have aroused him from his bed.
The mighty oak stands tall and strong, the wind sways its leaves in gentle song.
A squirrel sits on the forest floor, feasting on his nutty store.

A little stream quite happily sings, creating a chorus of violin strings,
Along its banks is a carpet of blue, the bluebell stands so tall and true.
So, walk in the woods, if they are to hand, you will be simply amazed at what inhabits that land.

Echo's

I can hear an echo calling, calling out your name.
The echo is getting louder as I begin to feel the pain.
Memories stir and waken as it increases in its pace
Then suddenly you are before me with a smile on your face.

It seems like only yesterday that I gazed into your eyes
But the echo is fading faster now as it takes away the prize.
I feel bereft and cheated, for once again you have gone.
I am left clutching at the memory for which I always long.

So, on this day I remember you and the echoes that still play
Within my heart and memory until my dying day!
So, when I hear you whisper and place your hand in mine
The echoes will be silenced until the end of time.

Age

Her eyes peek round the curtain grey
To face the world another day.
Alone the hours will slowly pass
Perhaps today she'll tread that path.

For ninety years this world has known
This wrinkled lady all alone
Her youth and blossom have been spent
And now her back is crudely bent.

The eyes like long lost sapphires were
Now are just a misty blur
The crowning glory on her head
Is now a knotted matt instead

Her tiny frame she moves from sight
There's not one else to share her plight
So up the stairs she climbs to rest
The cloak of death will do its best.

An age she's lived, an age she's died
And with her go her youth and pride.

Hope

Crashing wave on huge dark rocks
Then stillness on the shore
There lies before me a part of life
Yet I know there is much more.

The many forms beneath the sea
Yet I stand here alone
The freezing touch of man's cold hand
has turned my heart to stone.

As drawn breaks through with fiery gold
The world will wake once more
Another day has dawned on me
Perhaps an open door!

The Rain

The clouds move in, heavy with rain
They burst with their fullness onto the plain.
Patches of blue are scattered so thin
Nothing will stop the deluge, let it begin.

The sky looks so grey, so heavy with pain
The thunder roars closely, here comes the rain.
The noise is quite deafening as the lighting strikes home
But here I just sit, just watching alone.

Moonbeam

You said we would walk that moonbeam
That makes a path along the sea
That our journey would be together
But it was just not meant to be.

Anniversaries and birthdays they come, and then they go
And I want just to tell you that I still miss you so.
You walked that unknown journey the one we walk alone
And I have learned to live as one without you on my own.

It is so hard at times to remember US so much time has passed
But just know this my darling husband your memory will forever last.
The present is for me to live until we meet again
So, all my love to you today for forever it will remain.

Grandson

As the years roll by and you look back on this day
Archive your memories and in your mind let them play
I wish you love and kindness and that all goes to plan
As you step from your boyhood into a man.
You've always been special for your heart is so wide
I'm so proud of you that I'm bursting with pride.
The years fly too quickly and now this one's begun
Cherish it tightly, and remember the dreams that you've spun.
Let your heart lead you and don't be afraid to be strong
Follow your conscious and you'll never go wrong.

Childhood

The gentle clouds go rolling by, the sun peaks through an orange sky.
The catch is in and has been stored the fishing boats are firmly moored.
The silent village wakes from sleep another day for it to keep.
The white-washed houses blaze so bright until they fade with the cloak of night.
The children stretch their little legs and shake the sand from sleepy heads.
The sky has turned a sapphire blue with multitudes of things to do.
With longing eyes, they scan the shore their itchy feet will stay no more.
With wings on heels, they will run to their playground of the sea and sun.
Their laughter rings across the beach as tiny sand crabs try to pinch.
The sea will be their bath for now, the sun will be their fluffy towel.

The setting sun shows them the time and over rocks, they slowly climb.
The sand returns to sleepy heads and now they dream of comfy beds.

Pollution

This world we live in cries with pain, for man is determined it shall not remain.
For millennia it has been home to man, with glorious oceans and stunning land.
Yet man in his avarice beyond that known, pollutes the earth that is also his home.
Fossil fuels are a destructive invasion, filling the air with every equation.
When Earth had cooled enabling life, the air was pure the sky was bright.
Nothing marred our glorious home, but the thirst for fuel is destroying this dome.
We lived with candles, and warming fires, but now electricity is our desire.
Man has invented so many things, is there an answer that he can now bring?
Cherish this Earth for our children, and their children to come, let them live in paradise beneath the sun.
Let them breath pure air like it was before, there's nothing on Earth that we want more.

A Ruined Castle

The ruined castle sits on top amid the mountains on a hilly crop.
Thick green trees grow around, far above the distant ground.
Ribbons of roads far beneath, twist and turn in disbelief.
The castle turrets have fallen with age, it stands alone in a forest of sage.
In between these mountains tall, stands a dam whose water's fall
Into a lake so blue and clear with more mountains circling at the rear.
A river runs into a gorge, sculpting the rocks that time has forged.
The water here is dark and brown no sunlight reaches this far down.
A tiny bridge spans the river, its narrowness will make you shiver.
The air is crisp with such delight, no pollution to spoil this sight.

Flying in Your Dreams

Have you ever yearned to fly, soaring upwards in the sky?
Into the blue as if you have wings, looking down at the Earth at wonderful things.
The fluffy clouds that drift on by, resembling tablecloths in the sky.
A kestrel passes very near, his beady eyes do not bring you cheer.
Your arms outstretched you soar away, the sky is a wonderful place to play.
Other feathered friends look on take note, there is no sign of wings or cloak!
Far, far below a mountain range, reaches up so far, its peaks so strange.
The patterned quilt of fields below, the farmer has a lot to sow.
Tiny people walk on by you are invisible to the naked eye.
So when you wake up to the day, your arms do ache from so much play!

Natural Habitat

When you are far away from home
With a restless heart that longs to roam,
When you dream of her so fair
Close your eyes and you'll be there.
You'll bathe in pools as clear as glass
And dry your skin on velvet grass.
Your eyes will devour this beauteous land
And how you long to walk hand in hand, In England!
Shake off your foreign coat and come
To this land where your dreams were spun.
Where you spent your childhood years
Where the earth contains your salty tears.
Rise up come forth, and feast your eyes
On emerald hills and ochre skies.
Look through mine if yours are blind
With all her beauty so sublime, that's England!
With a stirring in your breast you'll find No peace until you rest, In England.

Spring

The willow bends with charm and grace
The breath of spring, her leaves embrace.
The crocus peeps with budding head
To greet the sun of gold and red.
The little spring with laughter plays
To greet the start of sunny days
The newest blades of grass push up
Along with hosts of buttercups.
The Ash and Oak will lift their heads
Too long they've slumbered in their beds.
An overcoat of green they'll wear
Their branches are no longer bare.
With every spring, the Earth awakes
With every dawn a new day breaks.
A swallow on a tilted wing
The beauty of every living thing, that's spring!

The Storm

The sky has turned so very dark, the clouds build in fury ready to spark,
The lightning cracks and hits the ground, lighting everything around.
The thunder roars with a deafening sound, the rain lashes hard at the waiting ground.
The wind is fierce bending the trees, bringing the branches to their knees.
The sea is furious crashing on rocks, the waves stand high like building blocks.
The current is racing and then drawing back, the noise resembles a whip as it cracks.
The clouds in the sky seem to bump into one, with no chance today of seeing the sun.
The noise is a crescendo of sound, sending debris flying which resides on the ground.
The promenade is empty today, not a sign of a child willing to play.
As the storm rages on it is frightening to see how destructive and strong nature can be.

A Mountain Range

The mountains rise with regal grace, a snow-capped top adorns their face.
A skirt of soft green moss adorns the rugged peaks that years have formed.
Halfway down there are craters bold, filled with icy water's cold.
The water is a deep blue-green, as clear as glass, or so it seems.
The granite sentinels reach to the sea, from whence they came, I do believe.
The waves crash with a mighty roar, to sculpt more details as in years before.
The peaks form shapes of beauty blind, older than man and his kind.
The clouds sit upon the top, draping down like a lacy cloth.
The beauty of such a rocky range has a magnetic force that is so strange,
It entices the soul to fly and soar, over its summit devouring more.

Solitude

Crashing waves on huge dark rocks then stillness on the shore,
There lies before me a part of life, yet I know there is much more.
The many forms beneath the sea yet I stand here alone,
The freezing touch of man's cold hand has turned my heart to stone.
As dawn breaks through with fiery gold, the world will wake once more.
Another day has dawned on me, perhaps an open door.

The Seaside

Summer is here and it's as hot as can be
People are glad to be by the sea,
The beaches are full of people galore
There really cannot be room for that many more.
Colourful deckchairs line up on the sand
In symmetrical patterns perfectly planned.
Shops selling candy floss and the pinkest of rocks
Are fast selling out of their bountiful stock.
Ice cream is seen dripping down small little hands
The seagulls stand watch hatching a plan.
Fish wrapped in batter and a dashing of salt
All served in newspaper just freshly caught.
Children build castles with buckets and spade
Their building is precise, and perfectly made.
The great British seaside is unique to us all
But give me the "Costas" paella and all!!!

Africa

It's a hot day on the Savannah, under the African sky
You can hear the lion's roaring and hear the meerkat's cry.
It has been a long hot dry summer and water they have not found,
They paw in desperation at the dry and arid ground.
The elephants follow their matriarch as she leads them to fertile ground
Her memory is implanted with past water holes she has found.
The Springboks do not dance and play the sun is just too hot today.
The monkeys screech into the sky their throats so parched and very dry.
The giraffe reaches into the trees to nibble on some dried-up leaves.
The leopard is draped on branches bare; he feels much cooler lying there.
The hippos wallow in the mud; it is much cooler for their blood.
As the hottest month has passed, they look for rain to give them grass,

The clouds start gathering in the sky, the cheetah looks up and gives a cry.
The sky has darkened and lightning forks, it hit the ground with a mighty force.
Then suddenly, the rain appears, it falls from clouds like blissful tears.

A Walk in the Country

When you walk down a lane in the countryside
You will often see horses their heads held with pride.
The rich golden brown of their coats as it sheens
Like mythical creatures, you could see in your dreams.
The hedgerows are thick with brambles galore
Ready for autumn when the fruits you can store.
Wild garlic is strong as it wafts through the air
You will find meadowsweet and nightshade, of the latter, beware.
Wild orchid and mallow grow perfectly well
Listen for the wings of the small pipistrelle.
A Hedgehog creeps slowly in the cover of night
A large toad croaks loudly with all his might.
So, when you decide to take a long country walk
Listen and watch, as the hedgerows can talk!

The Fairground

When the fairground comes to town, excitement buzzes all around.
The roller coaster its might so tall, creates loud screams from one and all.
It goes round the bends at a mighty speed, then drops to leave your shaking knees.
The ghost train frightens you so much when you feel wet dangly things that touch.
Shouts of horror are rendered in the gloom when ghostly visions appear to zoom.
The chairs that swing at an alarming rate, put you in a frenzied state.
The coconut stall is hard to pitch, the balls just bounce when you try to hit.
No coconuts here for little round eyes, there is nobody clever enough to win the prize.
The helter-skelter goes round and round until you finally reach the ground.
It leaves you dizzy and your head just spinning, but you must go back to the beginning.
The candy floss stall with its sugary sweet, is popular for small children to eat.

The aroma of onions hits the air, hot dogs are sold with hot mustard, beware.

The water chute brings screams of wetness galore, but still, they go back to suffer some more.

Calls of "roll up, roll up" ring in the air, when you're tired and broke, you leave the fair!

The Zoo

When you stroll through the zoo, there always seem plenty of things to do.
The tigers pace back and forth, if only they could really talk,
Their actions are indicative of frustration and gloom, hey! Just give me a bit more, extra room.
The chimpanzee's squabbles are so loud, its audible noise draws the crowd.
They are having a tea party but mostly throw the food around giving a show!
Other monkeys are safely caged, but they also scream with frightening rage.
The wolf paces around his tiny cage, his greying whiskers showing his age.
The elephants stand so tall and still, held against their mighty will.
The lions pace around their heads held down, the male has lost his rightful crown.
The sea lions are the only ones, who seem to be having any fun.
Fresh fish is thrown at them every day, they no longer have to catch their prey.
Is this right I ask aloud? But no one agrees within the crowd.

A Day at the Races

Wide-brimmed hats and some with veils, escorted by the men in tails.

The enclosure houses at centre stage, the horses that are on parade.

The horses' coats are polished bright, their jockeys are a colourful sight.

They have a job to keep them calm, with hand and voice to stop alarm.

There are tables spread with pure white cloths and shiny silver on the top.

Champagne buckets topped up with ice, are all sold at a hefty price.

The bookies call out loud and clear, their odds are shouted for you to hear.

The crowd is laughing with glass held high, the money bet would make you cry.

The jockeys lead their horses slowly, to the starting gate so they can go.

The crowd erupts with mighty cheers, the horses have raced this one for years.

The gate is up and they are off, heads held high, and tails aloft.

The horses' legs run mighty fast, chewing up the dirt and grass.

The roar of people standing at the fence is really deafening and so intense.

The mighty steeds approach the bend, delighted to see their challenging end.

The commentator shouts with excited glee, the winner has made it home and free.

Some people are jumping up and down, others are sad and simply frown.

Wide-brimmed hats and some with veils, escorted by the men in tails.

Look round to see their Rolls draw up; they get in laughing holding the coveted cup.

Nostalgia

Sitting by a glistening lake, staring at the sky
The sky is reflected in the lake, and you begin to wonder why?
You question what your purpose is? It is so unclear to me!
My random thoughts are so mixed up, as to whom I should really be.
I have worn many hats throughout my life, I have travelled far and wide
My professions are very varied, each a source of pride.
I am a mother and a grandmother; I have been a loving wife
But still, I question whether is there more to enhance this query in my life?
Is it normal for folks to sit and think your life has gone in just one blink?
They say that youth is wasted on the young; I suppose in a sense its true
Looking back, I recognise that person I once knew.

Dreams

What do you dream when you're asleep?
Are they dreams you'd like to keep?
Do you dream of mountains high?
Where you can almost touch the sky!
Or do you dream of those long gone
Of the faces for which you always long.
Of getting lost and cannot find your home
Of feeling that you will forever roam?
Of standing in the street quite naked now
Not believing your clothes have gone somehow.
Standing on a skyscraper tall
You freeze with fright in case you fall.
You keep edging closer toward the edge
Balancing precariously on the ledge
You topple over and then scream aloud
Your pillow acts as a fluffy cloud!

Down Under

There is a land far, far away
That started off in Botany Bay.
Life was harsh in those long days
People had a price to pay.
With sandy beaches and deep blue seas
It is now a popular place to be.
The surf is high if you should dare
For nasty things do linger there.
Sharks, stone fish, and men of war
Frequent these waters in their score.
Colourful birds fly into the air
Large spiders inhabit the houses there.
Christmas is extremely hot,
It is steaks on the Barbie and that is your lot.
Cute koala bears hide in the trees
Feasting on the eucalyptus leaves.
The kookaburra's laugh you will hear
Will make you smile from ear to ear.

London

Big Ben is found in the Elizabeth Tower
Its bell sounds loud at every hour.
The Houses of Parliament stands alongside
The mighty Thames flows with pride.
Tower Bridge is coloured blue
Its bridge lifts up to allow ships through.
Oxford Street with shops galore
Or Bond Street for a few pounds more?
In Piccadilly Eros stands proud and true
Will his arrow favour you?
Trafalgar Square with Nelson tall
Hold's magic galore for one and all.
The Lion's sit on the fountain's side
Their regal heads held high with pride.
Camden has a market long
With music in pubs for a "sing-along"
The cockney people have long since moved
To country pastures, Council approved.
The days of pie and mash are few
With jellied eels and liquor too.
London has now a different twirl
To the place I once knew when I was a girl.

The Sea

Have you ever swum under the sea?
The delights are so wonderful and incredible to see.
The fish are so varied, with spots and stripes
They will swim with you, it is such a delight.
Sea grass sways and dances with grace
A small sea horse swims out and you stare at its face.
It is incredible to see something akin to a horse
Its tail is in a curl, now did it just snort??
The coral is beautiful so coloured and rare
Its hues will delight you so please do take care.
A crab walking sideways is a hilarious sight
He scurries away with all of his might.
A stingray dances by so graceful when he swims
Beware of him though his tail holds a sting.
Jellyfish just float by with tentacles long
Again, do take care their sting is so strong.
Fish swim gracefully out of the rocks
They look like they are wearing beautiful frocks.
It is hard to capture the beauty you see
You wouldn't believe it is under the sea.

Look Upon

Look upon a starry night and choose a star for me,
I will take that star and clasp it tight for that is where you will be.
Look upon a bird in flight, with wings so strong and true,
I will look upon a bird in flight and in its strength see you.
Look upon a garden green and choose a bloom so rare,
I will look upon a garden green and see you standing there.
Look upon a forest green thick with trees that mighty stand
I will look upon a forest thick and have you in my hand.
Look upon a mountain blue with wispy clouds above,
I will look upon a mountain blue and know I have your love.